JAVASCRIPT

Easy JavaScript Programming For Beginners

Your Step-By-Step Guide to Learning
JavaScript Programming

Felix Alvaro

Acknowledgments

Firstly, I want to thank God for giving me the knowledge and inspiration to put this informative book together. I also want to thank my parents, my brothers and my partner Silvia for their support.

Table of Contents

Introduction

Hi there! Congratulations on acquiring this book. You have made a great investment in the attainment of new knowledge in the area of JavaScript.

My name is Felix Alvaro and I am an Internet Marketer, Entrepreneur and Author with the mission to motivate and inspire you to achieve your goals, by sharing my knowledge and experience through my books.

JavaScript is perhaps one of the most misunderstood programming languages out there. However, it is one of the most vital and most popular languages that can be found almost everywhere. The demand for JavaScript programmers is growing rapidly. Anyone that learns to master this vital component in programming, is set to have a bright future, whether that is as a career or for personal use.

It has been estimated that the demand for JavaScript programmers in the job market will be a staggering 22% higher by 2020 than what it was 5 years ago (2010). So, make sure you learn this skill, and learn it well.

Regardless of whether you are completely new to programming, or whether you are familiar with other programming languages, you have chosen the right guide to learn JavaScript. In this guide, I am going to teach you all you need to know, to make this language your *mother tongue!*

JavaScript is quite easy to write once you get the basics down. In this guide, I am going to break everything down for you in a simple approach that will enable you to grasp everything quickly.

5

I also don't assume you know something already and go into detail for every concept I teach.

In the first chapter, we will go over the history of JavaScript, what it is used for, and tell you all you need to get started.

Let's get to it!

Chapter One: Getting Started

In the first chapter, we will learn about the beginnings of JavaScript, what it can do, and the ways on how you can make the most out of this book.

History of JavaScript

JavaScript was not always what it is today. Created 2 decades ago (1995) by a guy named Brendan Eich within just 10 days. It started out as a language written 'on the back' of other popular languages, or in other words: written in a very similar manner to popular languages of that time.

When first released to the public, it had a very coffee-like name: 'Mocha', which was a name chosen by Marc Andreessen, the founder of Netscape. It was the company Brendan Eich was working for at the time. The name was soon changed to 'LiveScript' in September 1995 and then 3 months later trademarked under the clever name we know today: JavaScript. I call it clever because the name was chosen to resemble the 'Java' programming language that was very popular back then. Still today, many people think that JavaScript and Java are the same, which is not true.

JavaScript was then submitted to ECMA international, which was (and still is) the organization in charge of standardization of computer systems. In 1997, the language was approved and standardized under the name 'ECMAScript'; a name ridiculed by Brendan Eich. What this standardization meant was that ECMAScript would serve as the specification other web-browsers could implement.

Once introduced, JavaScript grew rapidly in popularity. Out of JavaScript, great programming breakthroughs were achieved. JavaScript's influence in other technologies like DHTML (dynamic HTML) allowed amazing features to be created, such as drop-down menus, pop-up windows and rollover buttons (button gets highlighted when you hover over it).

Today, JavaScript is one of the most generally utilized programming languages. It is supported by a big part of the major web-browsers, and used in web-design across the most visited sites in the world, like Facebook.com and Google.com.

Now let us take a step back and discuss what computer programming languages are, and why they exist.

Programming languages are used to give a particular set of instructions to the computer. However, computers don't understand our human-written instructions directly. Therefore, there is a 'translation' process that must take place.

What the computer understands is machine language, or 'machine code'. There are basically two ways that a programming language can be converted into the machine code that computers understand.

The first types of programming languages are called '*Compiled*' languages. The popular languages in this category are: C++, Java, C Fortran and COBOL.

A compiled programming language has to be coded (written) by the person doing the programming, and then this code has to be run through a particular program called a *compiler*. This 'complier' program then 'translates' the code into machine language, which the computer can understand, and then perform the given orders.

The second type of programming languages are called *Interpreted* languages. For example: JavaScript, PHP, Ruby, Haskell and Perl. With the Interpreted language, the code is still written in human form, but it is not necessary for the code to be run through compilers. Instead, the compiling (translation) process takes place in the actual browser, the moment the program is being run.

The benefits of these are that the process is shorter. Also, the programmer has the ability to update and make changes to the program at any time. On the contrary, because the program is being compiled and being run simultaneously, it can slow down the overall performance of the programs.

However, upgraded computer processers that operate faster, combined with JIT (Just-In-Time) compilers, have given a huge boost to the performance.

Today, JavaScript runs 80% as fast as compiled code, and it keeps getting faster.

To give an idea of how much easier our life is with code, here is machine code to write "hello world":

```
b8      21 0a 00 00
a3      0c 10 00 06
b8      6f 72 6c 64
a3      08 10 00 06
b8      6f 2c 20 57
a3      04 10 00 06
b8      48 65 6c 6c
a3      00 10 00 06
b9      00 10 00 06
ba      10 00 00 00
bb      01 00 00 00
b8      04 00 00 00
cd      80
b8      01 00 00 00
cd      80
```

With JavaScript it is as simple as:

```
alert("Hello World!");
```

Now I am sure you will agree that scripting is easier!

What can one do with JavaScript?

Nowadays, JavaScript is found in not only web browsers, but in applications, mobile devices, servers, and many other portable technologies. However, the most popular use of this script is in web browsers, where it is referred to as *'client side'* JavaScript. These run on web browsers and there you can use JavaScript to perform various tasks. Like I discussed before, there are some awesome features added to web-browsers through the use of JavaScript.

The most common uses that you will find on almost every site include the following:

- Drop-down menus
- Ability to drag and drop
- Having multiple web-pages within one window (Tabs)
- Creating lists that can be 'sorted'
- Input validation (for example, verify login details)
- Search suggestions
- Progress bars
- Various effects and much more

These are just a few common uses of JavaScript, but the list goes on. There is a lot that you can do with JavaScript, which is why it has become one of the most required skills for any web developer. Even though it is a vital skill, it is still very easy to learn.

Once you master the basic *syntax* - which are the rules that determine when and where to use certain symbols (such as the use of parenthesis to structure the code) – everything else is simply English language.

JavaScript is most commonly run on web-browsers, which are known as '*client side* JavaScript'.

With client side JavaScript, you are able to add interactive features to the browser in the following ways:
- By taking command of the browser itself, or making use of the functionalities of the browser
- By manoeuvring the structure and the content within the browser
- By controlling appearance of the browser, such as the font and layout
- By accessing information from different locations

To fully understand how one is able to achieve all of that, and manipulate web browsers, you need to have some level of understanding of HTML coding.

What Do You Need To Get Started?

Now, you may be wondering where you are going to be writing your program. Well before getting to the actual writing, I am going to take you through a simple set-up to get you fully equipped to get your programming gloves on!

Get the right browser

Personally, I like to use Google Chrome as it is a very simple to use browser and it operates very quickly. Even if you use a different browser at the moment, I urge you to install Chrome, as many of the lessons and tasks in this guide will be aimed at the Chrome browser in particular.

Installing Chrome is very simple:

1. Visit www.gooogle.com/chrome.
2. Select the correct version suitable for your PC and Click on *Download Chrome.*
3. Complete the Installation steps.
4. Done!

Now that you have a super-fast browser to run your programs, you now need an editor to actually write the codes.

This is known as a *source code editor*.

Installing a Source Code Editor

There are a number of awesome code editors that you can install for free. My personal favourites are Kompozer and Sublime Text.

Here is a list of the best code editors:

Editor Name	Compatible
Notepad ++	Windows
Text Wrangler	Mac only
JEdit	Windows and Mac
Crimson Editor	Windows only
Araneae	Windows only
Komodo Edit	Windows and Mac

I will be using Sublime text for the examples, but it should be quite similar on whichever editor you choose.

To install Sublime Text:

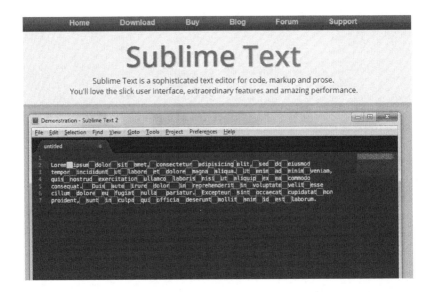

1. Visit http://www.sublimetext.com/.
2. Press *Download.*
3. Follow the install Wizard.
4. Move the application to your desktop for quick access.
5. Done!

When you open the application, it will look like this:

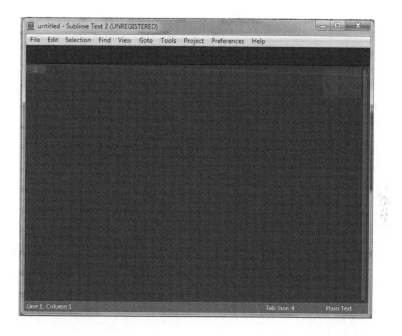

This is the basic layout for you to write your code.

A very helpful little feature is the side bar, that allows you to quick access all the files you have created and stored.

To open up the sidebar:

1. Click *View* from your toolbar.
2. Hover over *Side Bar.*
3. Click on *Show Open Files.*

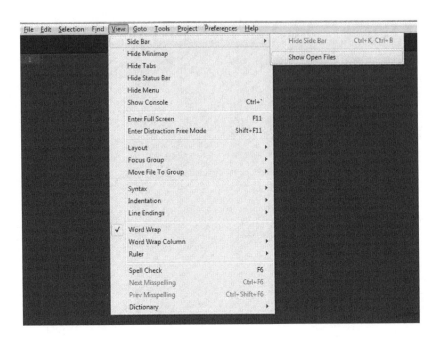

Now you should have a sidebar where you will be able to open up the files in your project.

Next, you want to begin creating a file and an appropriate folder in order to keep all the files organized in one place.

Follow these steps:

1. Select *File* and click *Save As.*

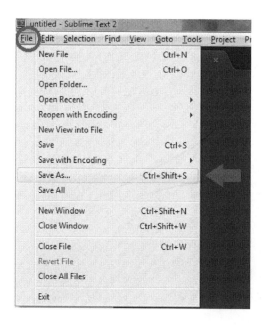

2. Find a suitable place to save your codes.
3. Create a new folder and title it '*JavaScript Project*'.

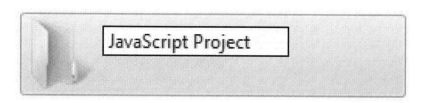

4. Open the new folder and save the file under *'JavaScript Program 1'*.

Nome file: JavaScrript Program 1|

Salva come: All Files (*.*)

:ondi cartelle

Salva   Annulla

5. Click *Project*, select *Save Project As* and select the new folder you created.

6. Save the project as '*First Project*'.

7. Select *Project* again and this time choose *Add Folder to Project.*
8. Find the folder you created named *JavaScript Project* and click *OK.*

9. The folder will then be added to your side bar that will also display the files you saved. This will give you better organization.

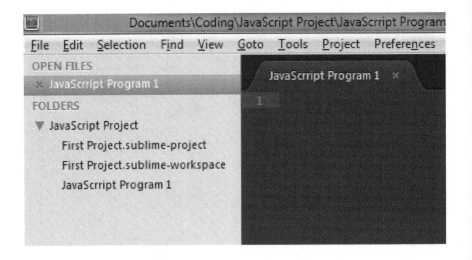

Now that we have the folders and files organized, I want to explain to you about the colour coding for your syntax codes.

The colour coding is set according to the type of code you write, look at the example below:

```
<!DOCTYPE html>
<html>
 <head>
<title>Make me a pizza</title> </head>
<body>
<script>
var pizza = {
meat:"",
cheese:"",
bread:"",
condiment:"",
makepizza: function (meat,cheese,bread,condiment) {
this.meat = meat;
this.cheese = cheese;
this.bread = bread;
this.condiment = condiment;
var mypizza = this.bread + ", " + this.meat + ", " + this.cheese + ", " + this.condiment;
return mypizza;
}
}
var pizzaOrder = pizza.makepizza("ham","cheddar","thin","hot sauce");
document.write (pizzaOrder);
var sandwichOrder = pizza.makesandwich("ham","cheddar","wheat","hot sauce");
document.write (sandwichOrder);
 </script>
 </body>
 </html>
```

1. You can always update a colour scheme you are more comfortable with by going to *Preferences*.
2. Click *Colour Scheme*.
3. Choose a colour scheme you prefer

Running a Program

Write the code below on your source code editor the let's have a look at your work by running the program on the web browser.

```
<!DOCTYPE html>
<html>
<body>
<script language="javascript"
type="text/javascript">
<!--
document.write ("This is my first code!")
// -->
</script>
</body>
</html>
```

To do so follow the steps below:

1. Save the code file that you have just created by selecting 'File' and then 'Save'.
2. Now go over to the Chrome browser.
3. Press Ctrl + O
4. Find the file you saved.
5. Open the file.
6. You should see the following displayed in your browser:

```
This is my first code!
```

If it doesn't appear this way, then you probably have made a minor mistake in the coding. Please go through it again and correct your mistakes and click File and Save again.

***

In this chapter, we have discussed the history of JavaScript, what the language can do, and the steps on how you can start programming. In the next chapter, we will learn about JavaScript and HTML.

Chapter Two: JavaScript and HTML

In Chapter Two, we will talk about HTML, how JavaScript is used within this framework, and the use of JQuery.

HTML

HTML stands for *Hypertext Markup Language*, which is a coding language that is used to construct and arrange webpages. It allows you to put all the elements of the page in place, from the placement of the images, the text used for headers, what the actual content of the page is, etc.

HTML Elements

A HTML page structures the content in what is called Elements. Elements are made up of an opening and a closing tag that are specified by the code and are used within angle brackets.

<openingtag>CONTENT</closingtag>

For example, to start an HTML document you must use the '<html>'. This tag lets the browser know that html code starts here and then it must be closed with a '</html>' to end the coding. Everything between those two tags will create one HTML Element.

To make it clearer, here is a basic HTML document with 4 of the most basic elements:

```
<!DOCTYPE html>
<html>
<body>

<h1>Heading Here!</h1>
<p>here is the content of the page displayed as
a paragraph</p>

</body>
</html>
```

The first tag, like we discussed, is the HTML tag. It appears in red in the picture above. Again, this tag is opened with <html> and closed with </html>.

Within that element, we have what we call a nested element. This is basically an element within another element. In the example above, you can see the <body> tag within the <html> tag which is where the content of the page would go. This tag is started with <body> and closed with </body>.

```
<body>

<h1>Heading Here!</h1>
<p>here is the content of the page displayed as
a paragraph</p>

</body>
```

Within the <body> tag, we can see a <h1> and a <p> element.

```
<h1>Heading Here!</h1>
<p>here is the content of the page displayed as
a paragraph</p>
```

The <h1> tags specify the main heading for the webpage which if you read my **#1 best-selling** book: "*SEO: Easy Search Engine Optimization, Your Step-By-Step Guide to a Sky-High Search Engine Ranking and Never Ending Traffic*", you would have learned that this tag can be very powerful for ranking a webpage highly on search engines.

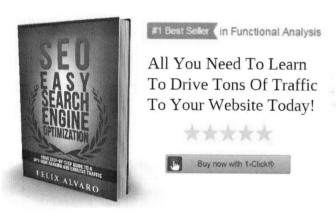

All You Need To Learn To Drive Tons Of Traffic To Your Website Today!

http://amzn.to/21HWFWb

Again, the heading is ended by entering the </h1> tag.

`<h1>Heading Here!</h1>`

Finally, the <p> tag is where a paragraph would start and then would end with a </p>.

```
<p>here is the content of the page displayed as
a paragraph</p>
```

Here's a simple table to make it easier to understand:

Content of the element	Start Tag	End Tag
HTML code	<html>	</html>
The page's content (i.e. blog post)	<body>	<body/>
Heading	<h1>	</h1>
Paragraphs	<p>	</p>

Remember: It is very important to not forget the end tag, as that can cause errors when displaying the content of HTML. There are even some tags such as the paragraph tag (<p>) that do not demand to be closed with a </p>, however don't run those risks.

Tip: It is also advisable to get into the habit of using lowercase letters within the tags. Even though not all versions of HTML demand lowercase tags, there are types of HTML, such as XHTML, in which lowercase letters is absolutely compulsory. Get into the habit early on and you won't have any problems in the future.

Elements may also contain additional information and these are called *Attributes*. Attributes are contained with the opening tag and are written in name/value pairs like: name="value". The values should always be placed in single or double quotation marks. The name is left unquoted and separated from the value with an equals sign.

For example:

```
<img src="my picture.jpg" width="106" height="148">
```

In the above picture, you can see the names are *width* and *height* and the values are *106* and *148*. These are the width and height of the pixels of the image.

Also, with the example above there is no closing <img> tag, as there is no content to be placed within the tags. All the content required to show that image is within the opening tag. However, I would still advise you to practice closing all tags as this will create good habits… don't try to cut corners.

There are a number of attributes that can be created, but we won't necessarily need to go into that right now.

Some essential attributes you should know:

Attribute code	What It Does
href	Used to specify a URL and should be placed in the <a> tag. For example: <a href="www.YourUrlHere.com">Click Here</a> The *Click Here* will serve as a hyperlink for the user to click on, which will direct them to the link within the quotation marks.
alt	Used to specify an alternative text for an image in case the HTML element cannot be displayed or to be read by screen readers. <img src="mypic.jpg" alt="Funny bunny picture"></img>
src	Used to specify the URL of the image displayed
title	Will provide additional information about an element which can be viewed as a tooltip.

Just remember the basics and you are ready to get started. The rest you will pick-up as you go along.

The beauty of JavaScript is that, if you are creating a webpage using HTML, you can very easily add JavaScript code to that document, or you also have the option of referencing the JavaScript file which will end in ".js".

As your browser runs, it will also run the JavaScript code found on the web page the user is viewing.

JQuery

JQuery is described as a "write less, do more" lightweight JavaScript library that works across most browsers.

Include the JQuery library to get started. Once installed, use the *jQuery* object to enable functionalities.

Syntax:

```
$("selector").method();
```

The first part (*selector*) signifies what elements you would like to change while the *method* part indicates the action that you want to perform to that element.

Selectors:

Selector	HTML Example	jQuery Example
element	`<p></p>`	$('p').css('font-size','12')
.class	`<p class="redtext"></p>`	$('.redtext').css
#id	`<p id="intro"></p>`	$('#intro').fadeIn('slow')
[attribute]	`<p data-role="content"></p>`	$('[data-role]').show()

After you make a selection, the next step is to start changing things. The three main categories for changes with jQuery are attributes, CSS, and elements.

The attr() method gives you access to attribute values. All that you need in order to use attr() is the name of the attribute whose value you want to get or set. In the following code, the attr() method is used to change the value of the href attribute of an element with an id of "homepage-link".

```
$('a#homepage-link').attr('href') =
"http://www.google.com/";
```

The result of running this statement is that the selected element's href attribute will be changed in the DOM to the new value. When a user clicks the modified link, the browser will open the web page at the specified address, rather than the one that was originally written in the img element.

Modifying an element using jQuery, changes only the element's representation in the DOM (and therefore on the user' screen). jQuery doesn't modify the actual web page on the server, and if you view the source of the web page, you won't see any changes.

jQuery makes modifying the style properties much easier than standard JavaScript, and the style properties are spelled exactly the same as in CSS.

Sample Code:

```
<html>
 <head>
<title>JQuery CSS</title>
<script src="http://code.jquery.com/jquery-
      1.11.2.min.js"></script> <script
      type="text/javascript">
      $(document).ready(function(){
```

```
$('#sizer').change(function() {
$('#theText').css('font-
size',$('#sizer').val());
}); });
```

jQuery features several methods for changing the content of element, moving elements, adding element, removing elements, and much more.

To get more tutorials and introductory lessons, visit https://learn.jquery.com/

***

In this chapter, we talked about HTML and JQuery and how JavaScript is used with these. In the third chapter, we will discuss JavaScript and CSS.

Chapter Three: JavaScript and CSS

In Chapter Three, we will discuss briefly about CSS, and I will give some basic JavaScript tips, for when you use it for browsers and websites.

CSS

Another vital skill you need to learn is CSS.

CSS stands for Cascading Style Sheets, which is language that controls the layout and presentation of a web page. It is used to dictate how different things should be presented. For instance, it will let you change colours, fonts, font sizes, backgrounds, the alignment of elements, borders and more.

This language makes it easy to make modifications without having to repeat the order for each element, unlike what you would have to do with HTML alone. Let me give you an example: if you wanted to change the colours of all the paragraphs to red, instead of coding each paragraph, you can use CSS and have all paragraphs changed.

Here is a CSS rule example:

```
p{font-color: red; font-family:
Arial}
```

In the image above, I have set a CSS rule that all p elements (which are the paragraphs), found within the HTML should be displayed in red colour, and in the Arial font. You simply place the element you want to target, enter the rules or properties within the curly brackets, specifying the desired change after the colon, and separating each rule with a semicolon.

That was a quick overview of JavaScript and the essential languages of HTML and CSS.

You will be learning a lot about HTML and CSS soon, so if you still feel a little bit confused, don't worry! We will be breaking down each step, in detail.

3 Ways To Run JavaScript in the Web-Browser

Like we discussed before, the most common place where programmers run JavaScript is on web browsers. To run JavaScript in the web browser, there are 3 ways that you can choose:

1. **Placing the script directly in the HTML event attribute**

The beauty of JavaScript is that there are easy to remember commands than can trigger the script based on an action. For instance, you can tell the browser to run the script once the page has finished loading by using the '*onload*' event attribute.

There are many event attributes that you can use, that will cause a script to be run according to the event attribute and the stimulation it requires.

Here are some of the most common event attributes:

Attribute	When used, the script runs...
onload	after the page finishes loading
onfocus	when element is focused on
onblur	when the element loses focus
onchange	when the value of an element is changed
onselect	when text has been submitted
onsubmit	when a form has been submitted
onkeydown	when a user is pressing a key
onkeypress	when a user presses a key
onkeyup	when a user releases a key
onclick	when a user mouse clicks an element
ondrag	when an element is dragged
ondrop	when a dragged element is being dropped
Onmouseover	when a user moves a mouse pointer over an element

I will add that using this strategy is not always the most recommended, or the easiest and most practical way of writing script. We will be covering better strategies soon.

2. Placing the script in an element (between a starting and ending tag)

This way of scripting is the most common and simply requires one to write the script in a similar way you would write other HTML codes, by writing it between a <script> HTML element.

This element should be written within a HTML document and is usually placed in the <head> element of the HTML.

Here is a simple example of what it should look like:

```
<html>
<head>
<script>(Your JavaScript code goes here)
</script>
</head>
<body>
Content here
</body>
</html>
```

Like the image above, the script goes in the <head> element (red) and is written using the HTML script tags (purple).

It can also be placed at the end of the body element. This is usually done if someone wants to have the script run after the page has loaded. Web browsers read just how we humans do, top to bottom. However, you don't have to place it at the bottom to have it run after the page has loaded, you can simply use the *onload* event attribute for this.

Here is an example of that event attribute:

```html
<!DOCTYPE html>
 <html>
 <head>
<title>Hello, HTML!</title>
<script>
        function countToThree(){
        var count = 0;
        while (count < 3) {
         count++;
        document.getElementById("theCount"
        ).innerHTML +=
         count + "<br>";
         }
        } Before Listing Code </script>
</head>
<body onload="countToThree();">
<h1>Let's Count to 3!</h1>
<p id="theCount"></p>
</body>
</html>
```

I would say that a downside of writing JavaScript as a HTML <script> element, is that you would have to continuously write and update that code on every page you want it to be executed.

If you are running a small or medium-sized site, this might not be so much of a big deal, but when you get to websites with a large number of pages, things start to get complicated.

This can be useful if you only have a one-page HTML site, as you would have one page to maintain and update. By writing JavaScript in the HTML, it allows your page to run faster and smoother. This translates to better user experience. But remember: be sure to not go overboard with the amount of script you code directly into the HTML document.

3. Write it in a separate document and place it in your HTML document

Search Engine Optimization or SEO for short, does exactly what the name says: optimize websites for search engines. It combines a number of different strategies, procedures, and actions that are used to increase website traffic organically, (in other words, unpaid), by tactically placing the website in the highest possible position in search engine results.

***

In this chapter, we discussed the application of JavaScript in CSS, and also learned about tips when using JavaScript in websites. In the next chapter, we will explore a basic JavaScript code and understand the syntax.

Chapter Four: Learning the Syntax

In this chapter, we will start to gain an in- depth understanding of coding with JavaScript. Let's start off by learning the basic syntax.

Sample JavaScript Code

Now it's time to break down a sample code, identify its parts, and become familiar with the syntax.

Here's a simple JavaScript code used in HTML:

```
<!DOCTYPE html>
<html>
<body>
<script language="javascript"
type="text/javascript">
<!-- This is a comment
document.write ("Hello World!!")
// -->
</script>
</body>
</html>
```

As you may have guessed, the output will look like this.

```
Hello World!!
```

Understanding the Basic Tags

These are the basic tags used in the code:

- **<!DOCTYPE html>** - Identifies the Document Type declaration. This is the standard value if using HTML5
- **<html>** - signifies that this is the start/end of the html document
- **<script>** - alerts the browser that the next lines should be interpreted as script
  Script attributes:
  - **language** – Signifies what scripting language you are using. However, newer versions of HTML (HTML5 included) have dropped the use of this attribute
  - **type** - recommended to indicate the scripting language. Value should be set to "text/javascript"

Line breaks and Spaces

Different to other coding languages, JavaScript does not take spaces, line breaks and tabs into consideration. The code will be read fine.

Only when you are writing actual English text that you want displayed on the webpage, do you have to aware of this. You may structure and format your code as you wish to make it organized and easy to understand.

Case-sensitivity

When reading (and writing) JavaScript, please be aware that it is case-sensitive. Be sure to enter the correct letter case.

In the example below, *firstName* and *firstname* are two different variables. Take extra care in writing variable and function names to ensure that your code will run properly.

```
firstName = "Anna";
firstname = "Mary";
```

Comments

Javascript recognizes the syntax for C++, C, and HTML comments.

```
<!DOCTYPE html>
<html>
<body>
<script language="javascript"
type="text/javascript">
<!-- This is a comment
document.write ("Hello World!");
// -->
</script>
</body>
</html>
```

HTML treats the following as comments:

- Any text between a // and the end of a line
- Any text between the characters /* and */ (this can be used for multiple lines)
- The HTML comment opening sequence <!-- (used for single line comment)
- The HTML comment closing sequence --> is not recognized by JavaScript so it should be written as //-->.

The Use of Semicolons

When writing JavaScript code, remember to always enter a semicolon at the end of each sentence. Your program is made up of sentences, or better said, statements. These statements combined are what create the result that you get from your coding. You must remember to always end each statement with a semicolon. If you do not, JavaScript will add one for you, and this can affect the results you get from the program.

***

In this chapter, we discussed about the basics of JavaScript syntax. In Chapter Five, we will start to go in full detail with variables.

Chapter Five: Using Variables

In Chapter Five, we will start off with learning about variables, a fundamental block in coding, and how they are implemented into JavaScript.

What are variables?

Think of variables as storage cabinets. Each cabinet is labelled with a name. Let's say we label it with *Dress Shoes*. Each cabinet contains one object – a pair of your old dress shoes, for example. If you have to put a pair of shiny, new dress shoes in the cabinet, you can take the old one out and replace it with the new.

Most programming languages, including JavaScript, use variables to contain data. These variables can be referenced throughout the code. In this chapter, we'll take a closer look at how variables are assigned and used in a code.

Data Types

When we say data type, this is the type of value that the programming language can support.

Unlike other programming languages, JavaScript is an un-typed language. This means that you don't need to provide the data type for a variable. JavaScript still distinguishes the different data types, but it can do the job on its own, without the specification from the code.

JavaScript supports the following primitive data types:

- Numbers – integers and floating- point values

- Strings – text, such as "Is this 1 line of string text?"
- Boolean – True or False
- NaN data type – Not a Number data type. This is the result when a math operation is done on a string, or when dividing by 0.
- Undefined data Type – when you create a variable and don't define a value for it, the default value is *undefined*

Naming Conventions

Before learning how to define variables, here are guidelines for naming your variables or objects:

- Variable names should not start with a number.
- Reserved words cannot be used. The list of reserved words is provided on page 47.
- As mentioned in the previous chapter, variable names are case-sensitive. Take note of what you are using.

Here's a tip: Before starting out with defining variables, develop your own style of naming convention. Make the variable name as descriptive as possible, but try not to make it too long. It should be descriptive enough so that when someone else looks at your code, he will know what the variable is for. This will also keep your code organized, structured, and easy-to-understand in case you need to troubleshoot.

For example: If assigning variables for names, you may use any of the two styles below:

FirstName	First_Name
MiddleName	Middle_Name
LastName	Last_Name

Be consistent with your style of variable naming and use it throughout your code.

Reserved Words

The following words cannot be used in any user-defined parameter (eg. objects, functions, variables, methods)

abstract	else	Instanceof	switch
boolean	enum	int	synchronized
break	export	interface	this
byte	extends	long	throw
case	false	native	throws
catch	final	new	transient
char	finally	null	true
class	float	package	try
const	for	private	typeof
continue	function	protected	var
debugger	goto	public	void
default	if	return	volatile
delete	implements	short	while
do	import	static	with
double	in	super	

Assigning a Value to a Variable

To use a variable, you must first declare it in the code.

We use the *var* keyword to declare variables.

Here is a sample of a variable declaration.

```
<script type="text/javascript">
<!--
var firstName;
var age;
// -->
</script>
```

Another alteration would be to declare both variables using the same var keyword, separated by a comma.

```
<script type="text/javascript">
<!--
var firstName, age:
// -->
</script>
```

Once the variable is declared, you can now assign or store a value to the variable. The process is called *variable initialization*. Following the example from above, the code will now look like this:

```
<script type="text/javascript">
<!--
var firstName="Mary";
var age;
age = 25;
// -->
</script>
```

In the example above, I've showed two ways on how you can initialize a variable. First, you can assign at the same time as you create the variable, or assign it anytime later in the code.

***

For this chapter, we examined variables, a basic building block in JavaScript. In the next chapter, we will continue with learning how to code using operators.

Chapter Six: Using Operators

In this chapter, we will discuss the heart of programs – operators and expressions.

Expressions are the lifeblood of a code. Expressions allow you to do arithmetic procedures, compare values, and assign values depending on conditions. For beginners, understanding how various JavaScript operators work is your first big step towards becoming a full-pledged JavaScript coder.

What are operators?

In the example **1 + 2 equals to 3**, the numbers 1 and 2 are called **operands** and the '+' sign is the operator.

JavaScript supports the following types of operators:
- Arithmetic Operators
- Comparison Operators
- Logical Operators
- Assignment Operators
- Conditional Operators

Let's discuss each type of operator.

Arithmetic Operators

Operator	Description	Example A=5, B=10
+	Addition (works for numeric and strings)	X = A + B: X=15 Y = "z" + B: Y = z10
-	Subtraction	X = A – B: X = -5
*	Multiplication	X = A * B: X = 50
/	Division	X = B/A: X =2
%	Modulus (outputs the remainder of an integer division)	X = B % A: X = 0
++	Increment by 1	X=A++: X = 6
--	Decrement by 1	X=A--: X = 4

Exercise: Here's a sample code using arithmetic operators:

```
<!DOCTYPE html>
<html>
<body>
<script type="text/javascript">
<!--
var x = 15;
var y = 12;
var z = "Strings";
var enter = "<br />":

document.write("x + y = ");
answer = x + y:
document.write(answer);
document.write(enter);

document.write("x - y = ");
answer = x - y:
document.write(answer);
document.write(enter);

document.write("x * y = ");
answer = x * y:
document.write(answer);
document.write(enter);

document.write("x / y = ");
answer = x / y:
document.write(answer);
document.write(enter);

document.write("x % y = ");
answer = x % y:
document.write(answer);
document.write(enter);

document.write("x + y + z = ");
answer = x + y + z:
document.write(answer);
document.write(enter);

document.write("x++ = ");
answer = x++:
document.write(answer);
document.write(enter);

document.write("y-- = ");
answer = x--:
document.write(answer);
```

```
document.write(enter);
</script>
<p> Practice using other variables </p>
</body>
</html>
```

Here's the output:

```
x + y = 27
x - y = 3
x * y = 180
x / y = 1.25
x % y = 3
x + y + z = 27Strings
x++ = 15
y-- = 16


Practice using other variables
```

Experiment with the values and change the variables.

Let's now move on to the next type of operators.

Comparison Operators

Comparison operators test for the validity of the expression and returns a value true or false value.

Operator	Description	Example A=5, B=10
==	Equality	A==B // false
!=	Inequality	A != B // true
>	Greater than	A > B // false
<	Less than	A < B // true
>=	Greater than or equal to	A >= B // false
<=	Lesser than or equal to	A <= B // true

===	Strict equality (checks for the data type)	3 === 3 // true
		3 === '3' // false

!==	Strict inequality (checks for the data type)	3 !== 3 // false 3 !== '3' // true

Exercise: Now, let's try these operators on our simple code:

```html
<!DOCTYPE html>
<html>
<body>
<script type="text/javascript">
<!--
var x = 15;
var y = 12;
var xx = '15':
var enter = "<br />";

document.write("x == y => ");
answer = (x == y);
document.write(answer);
document.write(enter);

document.write("x != y => ");
answer = (x != y);
document.write(answer);
document.write(enter);

document.write("x > y => ");
answer = (x > y);
document.write(answer);
document.write(enter);

document.write("x < y => ");
answer = (x < y);
document.write(answer);
document.write(enter);

document.write("x >= y => ");
answer = (x >= y);
document.write(answer);
document.write(enter);

document.write("x <= y => ");
answer = (x <= y);
document.write(answer);
document.write(enter);

document.write("x <= y => ");
answer = (x <= y);
document.write(answer);
document.write(enter);

document.write("x === 'x' => ");
answer = (x===xx);
document.write(answer);
```

57

```
document.write(enter);

document.write("x !== 'x' => ");
answer = (x!==xx);
document.write(answer);
document.write(enter);

</script>
<p> Practice using other variables </p>
</body>
</html>
```

Check the output if you got the correct results:

```
    x == y => false
x != y => true
x > y => true
x < y => false
x >= y => true
x <= y => false
x <= y => false
x === 'x' => false
x !== 'x' => true


Practice using other variables
```

Replace the values and explore the different combinations.

Logical Operators

Logical operators validate the truthfulness or falseness of the expression. The result of the expression evaluation will depend if one of them is true, both are true, or if a logical negation should be performed.

Operator	Description	Example X=true, Y=false
&&	Logical AND	X && Y // false
‖	Logical OR	X ‖ Y // true
!	NOT	!(X && Y) // true

Exercise: Using our simple code, let's see how these operators work:

```html
<!DOCTYPE html>
<html>
<body>
<script type="text/javascript">
<!--
var x = true;
var y = false;
var enter = "<br />";

document.write("(x && y) => ");
answer = (x && y);
document.write(answer);
document.write(enter);

document.write("(x || y) => ");
answer = (x || y);
document.write(answer);
document.write(enter);

document.write("!(x && y) => ");
answer = !(x && y);
document.write(answer);
document.write(enter);

document.write("!(x || y) => ");
answer = !(x || y);
document.write(answer);
document.write(enter);

</script>
<p> Practice using other variables </p>
</body>
</html>
```

Here's the output of the logical statements:

```
    (x && y) => false
(x || y) => true
!(x && y) => true
!(x || y) => false


Practice using other variables
```

Bitwise Operators

These are not commonly used in JavaScript. Not nearly as much as we use the other types of operators. We will discuss these operators in order, to have a complete understanding of what JavaScript can do.

When bitwise operators are used, the operands are transformed into their 32-bit binary representation, perform the operation, and convert the results back to decimal.

Let's take the value 12 for example.

This is 12 represented in binary:

00000000000000000000000000001100

Starting from the rightmost bit, each bit represents a value from 2^0-2^{31}. To represent 12, the 3rd and 4th bit are set to 1. This signifies a value of $2^3+2^2 = 12$.

The example above expresses a positive integer. To express a negative number in binary, we make use of the *two's complement* rule.

Let's convert -12 to binary.
The first step is to flip all the values.

```
00000000000000000000000000001100
11111111111111111111111111110011   // Flip
all values 0 to 1 and vice-versa
```

Next, add 1 to the result.

```
11111111111111111111111111110100   // Add
one to the rightmost bit
```

The above is the binary equivalent of -12.

Now let's have a look at what JavaScript can do with binary.

Operator	Description	Example A=3 Binary: 0011 B=2 Binary: 0010
&	Bitwise AND (Do Boolean AND on each bit)	C = A & B; C=2
|	Bitwise OR (Do Boolean OR on each bit)	C = A | B; C=3
^	Bitwise XOR (This means that either operand one is true or operand two is true, but not both)	C = A ^ B; C=1
~	Bitwise NOT (Reverses all the bits in the operand)	~A is equal to -4
<<	Left shift (In the first operand, all the bits in its are moved to the left by the number of places stated in the second operand. New bits are filled with zeros.	B << 1 is equal to 4
>>	Right shift (In	B >> 1 is equal

	the first operand, all the bits are moved to the right by the number of places stated in the second operand.)	to 1
>>>	Right shift with zero (Bit are shifted to the right, removing the bits that shifted off, and zeros are added from the left)	B >>> 1 is equal to 1

Exercise: Use the code below to demonstrate how to use bitwise operators. Manually solve the statements and check if you got the correct answer.

```
<!DOCTYPE html>
<html>
<body>
<script type="text/javascript">
<!--
var x = 2; // Bit 0010
var y = 3; // Bit 0011
var enter = "<br />";

document.write("(x & y) => ");
answer = (x & y);
document.write(answer);
document.write(enter);

document.write("(x | y) => ");
answer = (x | y);
document.write(answer);
document.write(enter);

document.write("(x ^ y) => ");
answer = (x ^ y);
document.write(answer);
document.write(enter);
```

```
document.write("(~y) => ");
answer = (~y);
document.write(answer);
document.write(enter);

document.write("(x << y) => ");
answer = (x << y);
document.write(answer);
document.write(enter);

document.write("(x >> y) => ");
answer = (x >> y);
document.write(answer);
document.write(enter);

document.write("(x >>> y) => ");
answer = (x >> y);
document.write(answer);
document.write(enter);

</script>
<p> Practice using other variables! </p>
</body>
</html>
```

Did you get it right? Here's the output:

```
(x & y) => 2
(x | y) => 3
(x ^ y) => 1
(~y) => -4
(x << y) => 16
(x >> y) => 0
(x >>> y) => 0
```

Practice using other variables!

Assignment Operators

Notice the parameter *result* in all of the sample codes above. The use of this parameter is an example of an assignment operator. Assignment operator assigns the value of the operand on the right to the operand on the left.

From our previous example, we assigned the value of **x &&** **y** to the parameter *result*.

```
answer = (x && y);
```

Here are other assignment operators:

Operator	Description	Example A=10, B=5
=	Simple Assignment	C = A + B; C = 15
+=	Add and Assignment	C += A (similar to C = C + A)
-=	Subtract and Assignment	C -= A (similar to C = C - A)
*=	Multiply and Assignment	C *=A (similar to C = C *A)
/=	Divide and Assignment	C /=A (similar to C = C /A)
%=	Modulus and Assignment	C %=A (similar to C = C %A)

Exercise: Do the exercise below to understand how assignment operators work.

```html
<!DOCTYPE html>
<html>
<body>
<script type="text/javascript">
<!--
var x = 22;
var y = 10;
var enter = "<br />";

document.write("Value of x =>(x = y) => ");
answer = (x = y);
document.write(answer);
document.write(enter);

document.write("Value of x =>(x += y) => ");
answer = (x += y);
document.write(answer);
document.write(enter);

document.write("Value of x =>(x -= y) => ");
answer = (x -= y);
document.write(answer);
document.write(enter);

document.write("Value of x =>(x *= y) => ");
answer = (x *= y);
document.write(answer);
document.write(enter);

document.write("Value of x =>(x /= y) => ");
answer = (x /= y);
document.write(answer);
document.write(enter);

document.write("Value of x =>(x %= y) => ");
answer = (x %= y);
document.write(answer);
document.write(enter);

</script>
<p> Practice using other variables! </p>
</body>
</html>
```

Did you get the output right?

```
Value of x =>(x = y)  => 10
Value of x =>(x += y) => 20
Value of x =>(x -= y) => 10
Value of x =>(x *= y) => 100
Value of x =>(x /= y) => 10
Value of x =>(x %= y) => 0
```

Practice using other variables!

Special Operators

There are other operators in JavaScript that don't fall under the categories mentioned above but are equally important to know if you want to learn how to code.

Operator	Description	Example A=10, B=5
?:	Conditional Operator (if condition is true? Then value X : Otherwise value Y	C= (A > B) ? less than value : greater than value C= greater than value
typeof	Typeof (evaluates the data type of the operand)	C= typeof A == 'string' ? this is string: this is numeric C= this is numeric

Exercise: Demonstrate the use of special operators.

```
<!DOCTYPE html>
<html>
<body>
```

67

```
<script type="text/javascript">
<!--
var x = 10;
var y = 20;
var z = 'z';
var enter = "<br />";

document.write("((x>y) ? 100:200) => ");
answer = (x > y)? 100 :200;
document.write(answer);
document.write(enter);

document.write("((x<y ? 100:200) => ");
answer = (x < y)? 100 :200;
document.write(answer);
document.write(enter);

answer = (typeof z=="string" ? "z is string":"z
is numeric")
document.write(answer);
document.write(enter);

answer = (typeof x=="string" ? "x is string":"x
is numeric")
document.write(answer);
document.write(enter);

</script>
<p> Practice using other variables!</p>
</body>
</html>
```

Here's the output:

```
((x>y) ? 100:200) => 200
((x<y) ? 100:200) => 100
z is string
x is numeric

Practice using other variables!
```

***

In this chapter, we explored the different JavaScript operators, and had our first few programming exercises. In the next chapter, we will continue to discover programming using loops, branches, and flow controls.

Chapter Seven: Designing Flow Control, Loops, and Branches

Here in chapter 7, we will explore the use of flow controls, loops, and branches to help us understand the decision- making process in a program.

Just like in real life scenarios, decision-making can be more complex than the usual *Yes/True* or *No/False* scenarios. In programming, not all scenarios can be evaluated using one-line statements. More often than usual, decisions can be reached after assessing numerous dependencies, and each output determines which path the program will take. This usually takes several lines of code to complete.

Now it's time to put what you have learned in the previous chapter into good use. In this chapter, we will use the different operators to define branches, flow controls, and looping statements.

Branches

Branches and loops are identified as control statements, mainly because these dictate the direction that a program goes.

If...Else Statement

If...else statements are used in a program to determine a path out of several possible options. These statements are used to determine different actions based on results of different conditions.

JavaScript supports the following if..else statements:

- if – used to assign an action if the condition returns true
- if...else – used to assign actions if the condition returns true or false
- if...else if... – used to assign an action for several conditions

Syntax:

If

```
if (condition) {
Statement to be executed if condition
evaluates to true
}
```

If...Else

```
if (condition) {
Statement to be executed if condition
evaluates to true
}else{
Statement to be executed if condition
evaluates to false
}
```

If...Else if...

```
if (condition 1) {
Statement to be executed if condition 1
evaluates to true
}else if (condition 2){
Statement to be executed if condition 2
evaluates to true
}else if (condition 3){
Statement to be executed if condition 3
evaluates to true
}else{
Statement to be executed if no condition
evaluates to true
}
```

Exercise: Use this exercise to validate the use of *if, if...else, and if...else if...* statements.

```
<!DOCTYPE html>
<html>
<body>
<script type="text/javascript">
<!--
var cost = 101;
var item = 'shirt';
var ans = 'yes';
var enter = "<br />";

if (cost > 100){
    document.write("<b> Price is more than your
budget. </b>");
    document.write(enter);
}
if (item=="food"){
    document.write("<b> This is necessary. </b>");
    document.write(enter);
} else{
    document.write("<b> Do you really need this?
</b>")
    document.write(enter);
}
if ((ans=="yes") && (item=="food")){
    document.write("<b> Then buy it.</b>");
    document.write(enter);
} else if(ans=="no"){
    document.write("<b> Then don't buy it. </b>")
    document.write(enter);
}else if(ans=="not sure"){
    document.write("<b> Sleep on it. </b>")
    document.write(enter);
}else {
    document.write("<b> Think about it. </b>")
    document.write(enter);
}
//-->
</script>
<p> Practice using other variables</p>
</body>
</html>
```

Output: Check your work. Did you get the correct output?

```
Price is more than your budget.
Do you really need this?
Think about it.


Practice using other variables
```

Replace the code with other conditions and explore what if...else statements can do.

Switch Case

The switch statement simplifies the *if..else if...* conditions when the output relies on the value of only one variable. Instead of using several lines of *if...else if...* statements, use *switch* instead.

Syntax:

```
switch (expression)
{
  case condition 1: statement(s)
                    break;
  case condition 2: statement(s)
                    break;
  ...
  case condition n: statement(s)
                    break;
  default: statement(s)
}
```

Exercise: Demonstrate the use of switch statement using the code below.

```
<!DOCTYPE html>
<html>
```

```
<body>
<script type="text/javascript">
<!--
var flavor = "pepperoni";

switch (flavor){
    case "cheese":document.write("Want some more
cheese?<br />");
        break;
    case "meat":document.write("One meaty goodness
coming up! <br />");
        break;
    case "pepperoni":document.write("Want anything
else to go with pepperoni?");
        break;
    case "vegetable":document.write("Try our salad
too!");
        break;
    default: document.write("Place your pizza
order first.");
}
//-->
</script>
<p> Practice using other variables</p>
</body>
</html>
```

Results:

```
Want anything else to go with pepperoni?

Practice using other variables
```

Loops

In programing, there are instances when your code has to perform one action several times. JavaScript makes it easier for us with the loop statements.

JavaScript supports the use of the following loop statements:

74

- while
- do… while
- for
- for…in

While Loop

The while loop is used to perform an action, as long as a condition is evaluated to be true.

Syntax:

```
while (condition){
    Statement(s) to be executed if
expression is true
    }
```

Exercise: Here's a simple code that shows how the while loop works.

```
<!DOCTYPE html>
<html>
<body>
<script type="text/javascript">
<!--
var count = 0;

document.write("Can you count to 5? Yes!
<br />");

while (count < 6){
    document.write(count + "<br />");
    count++;
}
//-->
</script>
<p> Practice using other variables</p>
```

```
</body>
</html>
```

Results:

```
       Can you count to 5? Yes!
   0
   1
   2
   3
   4
   5


   Practice using other variables
```

Do...While Loop

The *do...while* loop is similar to the while loop we've previously discussed, except that it checks for the condition at the end of the loop. The *while* loop checks the condition at the start, so if the condition returns false at the beginning, the loop will not be performed. When using *do..while*, even if the condition is false, the loop will be evaluated at least once.

Syntax:

```
do{
  Statement(s) to be executed;
}       while (expression);
```

Exercise: To clearly demonstrate and compare how *while* and *do...while* statements work, use the sample above and replace the variable *count* with a value of 6.

Compare this with the result of the code below.

```
<!DOCTYPE html>
<html>
<body>
<script type="text/javascript">
<!--
var count = 6;

    document.write("Can you count to 5? Yes!
<br />");

    do{
      document.write(count + "<br />");
      count++;
    }while (count < 6);
//-->
</script>
<p> Practice using other variables</p>
</body>
</html>
```

Results:

Result of while code with var *count=6*

```
Can you count to 5? Yes!

Practice using other variables
```

Result of do...while code with var *count=6*

```
    Can you count to 5? Yes!
6

    Practice using other variables
```

For loop

The *for* loop is ideal to be used in running codes for a fixed number of times.

The *for* loop uses the following elements:
- Loop initialization – Assign a starting value to a counter before the loop begins
- Test statement – Test if the condition is true. If the condition is true, the loop will be performed. If the condition is false, the evaluation will come out of the loop.
- Iteration statement – Increase or decrease your counter

Syntax:

```
for ( test condition; repetition
statement){
    Statements to be performed if test
condition is true
    }
```

Exercise: Use the sample code below to show how for loop works.

```
<!DOCTYPE html>
<html>
<body>
<script type="text/javascript">
<!--
var count;

document.write("Can you count to 5? Yes!
<br />");

for(count = 0; count < 6; count++){
  document.write(count + "<br />");
}
//-->
```

78

```
</script>
<p> Practice using other variables</p>
</body>
</html>
```

Result:

```
          Can you count to 5? Yes!
0
1
2
3
4
5


          Practice using other variables
```

For...In Loop

The *for...in* loop is used for looping through objects. Objects will be discussed further in Chapter 9. For the purpose of our discussion here, we will use an object to demonstrate how the *for...in* loop works.

Let's use the most familiar object that we have been using in the book so far, the *document* object.

Syntax:

```
for (variablename in object){
   statement or block to execute
}
```

Exercise:

```
<!DOCTYPE html>
<html>
```

```
<body>
<script type="text/javascript">
<!--
var anObject;

document.write("How for-in works <br />");

for(anObject in document){
  document.write(anObject);
  document.write("<br />");
}
//-->
</script>
<p> Practice using other variables</p>
</body>
</html>
```

Results: The code will show all the methods and properties within the *document* object. For simplicity purposes, results shown here have been truncated.

```
        How for-in works
location
fgColor
linkColor
vlinkColor
alinkColor
bgColor
all
captureEvents
releaseEvents
implementation
URL
documentURI
origin
compatMode
characterSet
charset
inputEncoding
      write
writein
...//results truncated

Practice using other variables
```

Flow Controls

In cases when you need your program to skip a block of code inside a loop, or to exit a loop completely, use the different flow controls in JavaScript.

- Break – to immediately come out of the loop
- Continue – to start the next loop iteration

Break

When we discussed the *switch* statement, the *break* statement was used to come out of the branching statement. Let's now use the *break* statement inside a while loop.

Exercise:

```
<!DOCTYPE html>
<html>
<body>
<script type="text/javascript">
<!--
var count = 0;

document.write("Can you count to 5? Yes!
<br />");

while (count < 6){
  if (count==2){
        break;
  }
  document.write(count + "<br />");
  count++;
}
//-->
</script>
<p> Practice using other variables</p>
</body>
</html>
```

Results: Notice that in this instance, the counting stops at 2.

```
        Can you count to 5? Yes!
  0
  1
```

```
        Practice using other variables
```

Continue

Use this statement to skip a block of code and start on the next iteration. All statements under the *continue* statement within the loop will not be performed if the condition is satisfied. The loop will go and start on the next iteration.

Exercise: Show how the *continue* statement can make the code skip actions.

```
<!DOCTYPE html>
<html>
<body>
<script type="text/javascript">
<!--
var count = 0;

document.write("Can you count to 5? Yes!
<br />");

while (count < 5){
  count=count + 1;
  if (count==2){
        continue;
  }
  document.write(count + "<br />");
}
//-->
</script>
<p> Practice using other variables</p>
</body>
```

82

```
</html>
```

Results: Notice how the counting skipped on 2?

```
        Can you count to 5? Yes!
    1
    3
    4
    5


        Practice using other variables
```

***

In this chapter, we explored the use of *if, else if, switch,* and *while* statements. Now, let's proceed in discussing bigger chunks of code and functions in the next chapter.

Chapter Eight: Using Functions

In this chapter, we will explore what functions are, how helpful these are in a program, and we will look into examples.

What are functions?

In huge programs, some parts will require performing repetitive tasks. In order to simplify this, JavaScript allows creating a *function*.

A function is like a program within your program that you can reuse anytime. Whenever your program needs to perform the same task, you can just call the *function*.

For example, we need to add the word *Yes* to several words in the program.

```
function sayYes(nameString) {
        nameString += " Yes";
        return nameString;
}
```

Whenever you need to do this task, you can call the function below:

```
sayYes("I will learn JavaScript");
```

When you perform this on the Java Console in your browser, the output should be similar to the one below:

```
"I will learn JavaScript Yes"
```

Using a Function

The syntax for defining a function is simple.

```
var myFunction = new Function() { };
```

You can also use the syntax below similar to the one we've used in the previous section:

```
function myFunction(){ };
```

When a function is defined, *parameters* should be stated.

```
function myFunction(parameter){ };
```

When a function is called, *arguments* should be passed to the function to satisfy the required *parameter*.

```
myFunction(myArgument);
```

Once a function has performed its task and you want to return the value from the function, you can use the *return* statement. This statement should be the last statement in the function.

```
return myValue;
```

If you define the same function twice in the code, JavaScript will allow and accept the definition. JavaScript will use the second function that you defined.

When you need to do the same task again in the code, you can just call the *myfunction* function and pass new parameters. In our first example using *addYes* function, you can just change the parameter to get new results.

85

```
addYes("I will be a good programmer");
```

Exercise: To fully understand and demonstrate your knowledge of functions, follow the exercise below. Paste the following lines in your browsers Java Console.

```
function concatenate(first, last)
{
  var full;
  full = first + " " + last;
  return full;
}
```

After pasting the code, call the function and pass arguments.

```
concatenate("Abby","Jimenez");
```

Results:

```
"Abby Jimenez"
```

Now go back to the code you just used. Remove the return statement and try to see what will happen once you call the function *concatenate*.

If you received the *undefined* value after calling the function and providing the arguments, you are on the right track.

***

In this chapter, we discovered how to simplify repetitive lines of code using functions. Next, we will delve into objects.

Chapter Nine: Using JavaScript Objects

In this chapter, we will discuss the use of user-defined as well as JavaScript objects. Let's begin by understanding what objects are.

What are objects?

JavaScript is an object-oriented language. Object-oriented means that the language is able to provide the following:

- **Encapsulation:** putting information such as data or methods, together in an object.
- **Aggregation:** storing one object inside another one.
- **Inheritance:** using other classes for some of its properties and methods.
- **Polymorphism:** writing one function or method that works in different ways.

Objects are composed of attributes. If an attribute contains a function, it is considered to be a method of the object. Otherwise, the attribute is considered a property.

To understand JavaScript objects and its components, let's compare it to a real-world object. Let's use a car for example.

The following are the things that describe my car:
- It is a compact sedan
- Its color is silver
- It can fit 5 people

Some of the things that my car does are:

- For personal needs, drive to work
- For errands, drive my pet to the vet clinic
- For vacation, drive to the beach

In JavaScript terms, the things that describe my car are the *object properties*. The things that my car does or the things that I use my car for are called *object methods*.

Both methods and properties are written as name-value pairs, using a colon to separate the name and value. Methods are properties that contain functions as values.

This is how it would look if we turn my car into a JavaScript object:

```
var car = {
        carColor: "silver",
        carType: "Compact Sedan",
        passengers: 5,
        errands: function() {...},
        vacation: function() {...}
        personal: function() {...}
};
```

Creating an object

There are two ways to create a JavaScript object:
1. Using object literal
2. Using the object constructor method

Using Object Literal

The object literal method uses the *var* keyword similar to defining a variable.

```
var dog = {name: "Abby", eyeColor: "brown",
age: 7};
```

Also, similar to defining variables, you can define the object first and add the properties at a later time.

```
var dog = {};
dog.name= "Abby";
dog.eyeColor= "brown";
dog.age= 7;
```

Using Object Constructor

This uses the *Object* method to create an object and add properties.

```
var dog = new Object();
dog.name= "Abby";
dog.eyeColor= "brown";
dog.age= 7;
```

Between these two methods, using the object literal method is more recommended to use, because the Object constructor method does not perform well in web browsers and are more complex to read than the object literal method.

All user-defined objects are descendants of the object *object*.

Understanding Methods

As mentioned earlier in this chapter, methods are properties that contain functions as values. Methods are defined similar to the way functions are defined.

The main difference between a function and a method is that the former is a stand-alone unit while the latter is attached to an object and can be referenced by the *this* keyword.

```
var pizza = {
meat:"",
cheese:"",
bread:"",
condiment:"",
makepizza: function
(meat,cheese,bread,condiment) {
pizza.meat = meat;
pizza.cheese = cheese;
pizza.bread = bread;
pizza.condiment = condiment;
var mypizza = pizza.bread + ", " +
pizza.meat + ", " + pizza.cheese + ", " +
pizza.condiment;
return mypizza;
} }
```

Exercise: Use the code below to demonstrate how an object works.

```
<html>
 <head>
<title>Make me a pizza</title> </head>
<body>
<script>
var pizza = {
meat:"",
cheese:"",
bread:"",
condiment:"",
makepizza: function
(meat,cheese,bread,condiment) {
pizza.meat = meat;
pizza.cheese = cheese;
```

```
        pizza.bread = bread;
        pizza.condiment = condiment;
        var mypizza = pizza.bread + ", " +
pizza.meat + ", " + pizza.cheese + ", " +
pizza.condiment;
        return mypizza;
        } }
        var pizzaOrder =
pizza.makepizza("ham","cheddar","thick","hot
sauce");
        document.write (pizzaOrder);
          </script>
        </body>
        </html>
```

Results:

```
thick, ham, cheddar, hot sauce
```

Using 'this' Keyword

The *this* keyword is a shorthand to referring to the object being passed to the function.

```
<!DOCTYPE html>
<html>
  <head>
<title>Make me a pizza</title> </head>
<body>
<script>
var pizza = {
meat:"",
cheese:"",
bread:"",
condiment:"",
makepizza: function
(meat,cheese,bread,condiment) {
this.meat = meat;
this.cheese = cheese;
this.bread = bread;
this.condiment = condiment;
var mypizza = this.bread + ", " + this.meat +
", " + this.cheese + ", " + this.condiment;
return mypizza;
} }
```

91

```
var pizzaorder =
pizza.makepizza("ham","cheddar","thin","hot
sauce");
document.write (pizzaorder);
  </script>
  </body>
  </html>
```

In the code above, all *makepizza* object was replaced with
this to refer to the object.

Javascript Objects

In this section, we will look into samples of JavaScript
objects and their methods.

When writing your own code, you can simply use and reuse
these objects, depending on the functionality that you need.

String Object

The *string* object allows developers to work on characters.

Syntax: Use the syntax below to create a string object.

```
var val = new String(string);
```

Here is the list of methods for *string* object and the specific
return values:

Method	Description
charAt()	Outputs the character at the specified index
charCodeAt()	Outputs the number indicating the

	Unicode value of the character
concat()	Combines the text of two strings and returns a new string.
indexOf()	Ouputs the index within the calling String object of the first instance of the value
localeCompare()	Ouputs the number indicating if a reference string comes before or after
match()	Match a regular expression against a string
replace()	Find a match between a regular expression and a string, and to replace the matched string with a new string.
search()	Search for a match between a regex and a specified string.
slice()	Cut a section of a string and returns a new string.
split()	Splits a String into an array of strings
substr()	Characters in a string beginning at the specified location through the specified number of characters.
substring()	Characters in a string between two indexes
toLocaleLowerCase()	Convert characters to lower case while keeping the current locale.
toLocaleUpperCase()	Convert characters to upper case while keeping the current locale.
toLowerCase()	Convert calling string value to lower case.
toString()	String representing the specified object.
toUpperCase()	Convert calling string value to upper case.

Exercise: Practice with the codes below, to demonstrate how to use some methods of the *string* object.

charAt()

Returns the character at a particular index.

Syntax:
```
string.charAt(index)
```

Argument Details:

index: integer between 0 and 1 less than the length of the string.

Return Value:
Returns the character from the specified index.

Sample Code:

```
<html>
<head>
<title>JavaScript String charAt()
Method</title> </head>
<body>
<script type="text/javascript">
      var string1 = new String( "This is
      string" );
      document.writeln("string1.charAt(0
      ) is:" + str.charAt(0));
      document.writeln("<br
      />string1.charAt(1) is:" +
      string1.charAt(1));
      document.writeln("<br />
      string1.charAt(2) is:" +
      str.charAt(2));
      document.writeln("<br />
      string1.charAt(3) is:" +
      string1.charAt(3));
      document.writeln("<br />
```

```
        string1.charAt(4) is:" +
        string1.charAt(4));
        document.writeln("<br
        />v.charAt(5) is:" +
        string1.charAt(5));
</script>
</body>
</html>
```

Results:

```
String1.charAt(0) is:T
String1.charAt(1) is:h
String1.charAt(2) is:i
String1.charAt(3) is:s
String1.charAt(4) is:
String1.charAt(5) is:i
```

concat()

Adds strings and returns a new single string.

Syntax:
```
string.concat(string1, string2, ...,
stringN);
```

Argument Details:

   string2...stringN: strings that you want to
join.

Return Value:

One concatenated string.

Sample Code:

```
<html>
<head>
<title> concat Method</title> </head>
<body>
<script type="text/javascript">
      var string1 = new String( "This is
string 1" );
      var string2 = new String( "This is
String 2" );
      var string3 = string1.concat(
string2 );
      document.write("New joined String
:" + string3); </script>
</body>
</html>
```

Results:

```
New joined String :This is String 1 This
is String 2
```

indexOf()

Returns the index of the first instance of the
specified value. Returns -1 if the value is not found.

Syntax:

```
string.indexOf(searchValue[, fromIndex])
```

Argument Details:

      searchValue: string denoting the value you
are searching for
      fromIndex: location to start the search. Use
any integer between 0 and the length of the string.
The default value is 0.

Return Value:

index of the found occurrence, otherwise -1 if not found.

Sample Code:

```
<html>
<head>
<title> indexOf Method</title>
</head>
<body>
<script type="text/javascript">
var string1 = new String( "This is string one" );
var index = string1.indexOf( "string" );
document.write("indexOf found String :" + index );
        document.write("<br />");
var index = string1.indexOf( "one" );
document.write("indexOf found one :" + index );
</script>
</body>
</html>
```

Results:

```
indexOf found String :8
indexOf found one :15
```

replace()

Finds a match between a regular expression and a string, and replaces the matched string with a new string.

97

This can include the following patterns:

$$ - Inserts a "$"
$& - Inserts the matched substring
$` - Inserts the portion of the string that precedes the matched substring
$' - Inserts the portion of the string that follows the matched substring
$n or $nn **n** or **nn** are decimal digits, inserts **n**th parenthesized submatch string, provided the first argument was a RegExp object

Syntax:

```
string.replace(regular
expression/string, new string/function[,
flags]);
```

Argument Details:

   regexp : Regexp. The match is replaced by the return value of parameter #2.
   substr : String that is to be replaced by new string.
   newSubStr : String that should replace the string received from parameter #1.
   function : called to create the new string.
   flags : g - global match, i - ignore case, m - match over multiple lines.

Return Value:

The changed string

Sample Code:

```
<html>
<head>
<title> replace Method</title>
</head>
<body>
<script type="text/javascript">
        var re = /oranges/gi;
    var string1 = "oranges are
delicious, and oranges are good for your
health.";
    var newstring =
string1.replace(re, "apples");
        document.write(newstr );
</script>
</body>
</html>
```

Results:

```
apples are delicious, and apples are
good for your health
```

search()

Search for a match between a reg ex and this
String object.

Syntax:

```
string.search(regexp);
```

Argument Details:

regexp : regular expression object.

Return Value:

search returns the index of the regular expression inside the string. Otherwise, it returns -1.

Sample Code:

```
<html>
<head>
<title> search Method</title>
</head>
<body>
<script type="text/javascript">
var search1 = /Baskets/gi;
var string1 = "Baskets are round,
and Baskets are heavy.";
if ( str.search(search1) == -1 ){
     document.write("Does not
contain Baskets" );
}else{
document.write("Contains Baskets"
);
}
</script>
</body>
</html>
```

Results:

```
Contains Baskets
```

Date Object

This is a datatype built into the JavaScript language. Date objects are created with the new Date() object as shown below.

Syntax: You can use any of the syntax below to create a Date object using *Date ()* constructor.

```
new Date( )
new Date(milliseconds)
new Date(datestring)
new
Date(year,month,date[,hour,minute,second,milli
second ])
```

Here are the methods applicable for *date* object.

Method	Description
Date()	Outputs the current date, including time
getDate()	Outputs the day
getDay()	Outputs the day of the week in the parameter
getFullYear()	Outputs the year in the parameter
getHours()	Outputs the Hour in the parameter
getMilliseconds()	Outputs the milliseconds in the parameter
getMinutes()	Outputs the minutes in the parameter
getMonth()	Outputs the month in the parameter
getSeconds()	Outputs the Seconds in

		the parameter
	getTime()	Outputs the numeric value of the specified date represented as the number of milliseconds since January 1, 1970, 00:00:00 UTC.
)	getTimezoneOffset(	Outputs the time-zone offset in minutes
	getUTCDate()	Outputs the Day (date) of the month in the parameter according to UTC
	getUTCDay()	Outputs the Day of the week in the parameter according to UTC
	getUTCFullYear()	Outputs the year in the parameter according to UTC
	getUTCHours()	Outputs the Hours in the parameter according to UTC
s()	getUTCMillisecond	Outputs the Milliseconds in the parameter according to UTC
	getUTCMinutes()	Outputs the Minutes in the parameter according to UTC
	getUTCMonth()	Outputs the Month in the parameter according to UTC
		Outputs the Seconds in the parameter according to

getUTCSeconds()	UTC
setDate()	Assigns the day of the month in the parameter
setFullYear()	Assigns the year in the parameter
setHours()	Assigns the hours in the parameter
setMilliseconds()	Assigns the milliseconds in the parameter
setMinutes()	Assigns the minutes in the parameter
setMonth()	Assigns the month in the parameter
setSeconds()	Assigns the seconds in the parameter
setTime()	Assigns the Date object to the time represented by a number of milliseconds since January 1, 1970, 00:00:00 UTC.
setUTCDate()	Assigns the day of the month according to UTC
setUTCFullYear()	Assigns the full year according to UTC

	setUTCHours()	Assigns the hour according to UTC
s()	setUTCMillisecond	Assigns the milliseconds according to UTC
	setUTCMinutes()	Assigns the minutes in the parameter according to universal time.
	setUTCMonth()	Assigns the month according to UTC
	setUTCSeconds()	Assigns the seconds according to UTC
	toDateString()	Converts the date section of the Date as readable string
()	toLocaleDateString	Converts the date section of the Date as a string, using the current conventions.
	toLocaleFormat()	Converts a date to a string
	toLocaleString()	Converts a date to a string, using the current conventions
()	toLocaleTimeString	Converts the time section of the Date as a string, using the current conventions.
	toSource()	A string representing the source for an equivalent Date

	object
toString()	A string representing the specified Date object.
toTimeString()	Converts and outputs the time section of the Date as string.
toUTCString()	Converts a date to a string, using UTC convention
valueOf()	Primitive value of a Date object.

Exercise: Practice with the codes below to demonstrate how to use some methods of the *date* object.

Date()

Today's date and time

Syntax:

```
Date ()
```

Return Value:

Today's date and time

Sample Code:

```
<html>
<head>
<title> Date </title> </head>
<body>
```

```
<script type="text/javascript">
   var datetime = Date();
   document.write("Date-Time : " +
datetime ); </script>
   </body>
   </html>
```

Results:

```
   Date-Time : Wed Jan 25 2016 15:00:57
GMT+0800 (Hongkong Standard Time)
```

getDate()

The day of the month for the specified date according to local time.

Syntax:

```
Date.getDate()
```

Return Value:

Day of the month for the specified date.

Sample Code:

```
   <html>
   <head>
   <title> getDate </title> </head>
   <body>
   <script type="text/javascript">
   var datetime = new Date("January
27, 2016 23:15:00");
   document.write("getDate() : " +
datetime.getDate() );
</script>
   </body>
   </html>
```

Results:

```
getDate() : 27
```

getDay()

Day of the week for the specified date according to local time. Value is an integer corresponding to the day of the week: 0 – Sunday, 1 – Monday, 2- Tuesday, 3- Wednesday, 4- Thursday, 5- Friday, and 6 – Saturday.

Syntax:

```
Date.getDay()
```

Return Value:

Day of the week for the specified date.

Sample Code:

```html
<html>
<head>
<title> getDate </title> </head>
<body>
<script type="text/javascript">
    var datetime = new Date("January
27, 2016 23:15:00");
    document.write("getDate() : " +
datetime.getDate() );
</script>
</body>
</html>
```

Results:

```
getDate() : 27
```

getTime()

Numeric value corresponding to the time of the specified date according to UTC. The number returned is the number of milliseconds from specified date to January 1, 1970.

Syntax:

```
Date.getTime()
```

Return Value:

Millisecond value corresponding to the specified date in relation to UTC.

Sample Code:

```
<html>
<head>
<title> getTime </title> </head>
<body>
<script type="text/javascript">
    var datetime = new Date( "February
9, 2016 05:30:38" );
    document.write("getTime() : " +
datetime.getTime() );
</script>
</body>
</html>
```

Results:

```
getTime() : 1455010238000
```

setDate()

Sets the day of the month

Syntax:

```
Date.setDate( day )
```

Argument Details:

day : An integer from 1 to 31

Return Value:

Sets the day

Sample Code:

```
<html>
<head>
<title> setDate </title> </head>
<body>
<script type="text/javascript">
  var datetime = new Date( "Aug 25,
2010 23:30:00" );
  datetime.setDate( 24 );
  document.write( dt );
</script>
</body>
</html>
```

109

Results:

```
Sun Aug 25 2010 23:30:00 GMT+0800
(Hongkong Standard Time)
```

setHours()

Sets the hours for a specified date according to local time

Syntax:

```
Date.setHours(hours[, minutes [, seconds [, ms]]])
```

Argument Details:

    hours : Represents the hour, Any value between 0 and 23

    minutes : Represents the minutes, any value between 0 and 59

    seconds : Represents the seconds, any value between 0 and 59. If you declare the seconds parameter, you must also include minutes.

    ms : Represents milliseconds, any value between 0 and 999. If you declare the ms parameter, you must also specify the minutes and seconds.

    If no values are declared for minutes, seconds, and ms, then the values returned from *getUTCminutes*, *getUTCseconds,* and *getmilliseconds* will be used.

Sample Code:

```
<html>
<head>
<title> setHours Method</title>
</head>
<body>
<script type="text/javascript">
var datetime = new Date( "Aug 25,
2010 23:30:00" );
datetime.setHours( 02 );
document.write( datetime );
</script>
</body>
</html>
```

Results:

```
Thu Aug 25 2010 02:30:00 GMT+0800
(Hongkong Standard Time)
```

toDateString()

Outputs and converts the Date section of a Date in readable form

Syntax:

```
Date.toDateString()
```

Sample Code:

```
<html>
<head>
<title> setHours </title> </head>
<body>
<script type="text/javascript">
  var datetime = new Date(2001, 6,
25, 13, 12, 7);
  document.write( "Formatted Date :
" + datetime.toDateString() );
</script>
</body>
</html>
```

Results:

```
Formatted Date : Wed Jul 25 2001
```

toString()

Returns a string representing the specified Date
object

Syntax:

```
Date.toString ()
```

Sample Code:

```
<html>
<head>
<title>JavaScript setHours
Method</title> </head>
<body>
<script type="text/javascript">
var dateobject = new Date(2002, 6,
15, 20, 14, 7);
stringobject =
dateobject.toString();
document.write( "String: " +
stringobject );
</script>
</body>
</html>
```

Results:

```
String: Wed Jul 15 2002 20:14:07 GMT+0800
(Hongkong Standard Time)
```

Math Object

You will find mathematical constants and functions using the *math* object. Unlike other global objects, *Math* is not a constructor, so all the properties and methods of Math are constant and can be called by using Math as an object.

Use the constant pi as Math.PI and call the tangent function as Math.tan(x).

Method	Description
abs()	Outputs the absolute value
acos()	Outputs the arccosine (in radians)
asin()	Outputs the arcsine (in radians)
atan()	Outputs the arctangent (in radians)
atan2()	Outputs the arctangent of the quotient of its arguments.
ceil()	Outputs the smallest integer
cos()	Outputs the cosine

exp()	Outputs natural logarithm E^N, where N is the argument, and E is Euler's constant
floor()	Outputs the largest integer
log()	Outputs the natural logarithm (base E)
max()	Outputs the largest number
min()	Outputs the smallest number
pow()	Outputs base to the exponent power,
random()	Outputs a pseudo-random number between 0 and 1.
round()	Outputs the value of a number rounded off to the nearest integer.
sin()	Outputs the sine
sqrt()	Outputs the square root
tan()	Outputs the tangent
toSource()	Outputs the string "Math".

Exercise: Practice with the codes below to demonstrate how to use some methods of the *date* object.

cos()

Cosine of a number.

Syntax:

```
Math.cos (x)
```

Return Value:

Cosine of a number

Sample Code:

```
<html>
<head>
<title> Math cos()</title> </head>
<body>
<script type="text/javascript">
    var mathvalue = Math.cos(90);
document.write("First Value : " +
mathvalue );
    var mathvalue = Math.cos(30);
    document.write("<br />Second Value
: " + mathvalue);
    var mathvalue = Math.cos(-1);
    document.write("<br />Third Value
: " + mathvalue);
    var mathvalue =
Math.cos(2*Math.PI);
    document.write("<br />Fourth Value
: " + mathvalue); </script>
</body>
</html>
```

Results:

```
First Value : -0.4480736161291702
Second Value : 0.15425144988758405
Third Value : 0.5403023058681398
Fourth Value : 1
```

floor()

Largest integer less than or equal to a number

Syntax:

```
Math.floor (x)
```

Return Value:

largest integer less than or equal to a number

Sample Code:

```html
<html>
<head>
<title> Math floor()</title> </head>
<body>
<script type="text/javascript">
     var mathvalue = Math.floor(10.3);
document.write("First Value : " +
mathvalue);
     var mathvalue = Math.floor(30.9);
     document.write("<br />Second Value
: " + mathvalue);
     var mathvalue = Math.floor(-2.9);
     document.write("<br />Third Value
: " + mathvalue);
     var mathvalue = Math.floor(-2.2);
     document.write("<br />Fourth Value
: " + mathvalue); </script>
</body>
</html>
```

117

Results:

```
First Value : 10
Second Value : 30
Third Value : -3
Fourth Value : -3
```

max()

Outputs the largest number; If no arguments are provided, the result is **–Infinity.**

Syntax:

```
    Math.max(value1, value2, ... valueX
) ;
```

Return Value:

Returns the largest number

Argument Details:

value1, value2, ... valueX : Numbers.

Sample Code:

```
<html>
<head>
<title> max()</title> </head>
<body>
<script type="text/javascript">
      var mathvalue = Math.max(10, 20, -
1, 100); document.write("First
Value : " + value );
      var mathvalue = Math.max(-1, -3, -
40); document.write("<br />Second value
: " + mathvalue);
      var mathvalue = Math.max(0, -1);
      document.write("<br />Third Value
: " + mathvalue);
     var value = Math.max(100);
      document.write("<br />Fourth Value
: " + mathvalue); </script>
</body>
</html>
```

Results:

```
First Value : 100
Second Value : -1
Third Value : 0
Fourth Value : 100
```

***

In this chapter, we explored what objects are, its parts, and how it is created. We also talked about some important JavaScript objects that we can use in coding. In the next chapter, we will take a closer look at the *array* object.

Chapter Ten: Working with Arrays

In Chapter Ten, we will go into an in-depth understanding of the *array* object and how it can be used in our code. We will also identify the different properties and methods of an array.

What is an array?

A parameter can have a list of values. Take, for example, the variable *color*. The values for these are red, blue, and yellow. Instead of defining a variable for each (eg. *color1=red, color2=blue, color3=yellow*), we use arrays to simplify the way we store multiple values or lists of values in a variable.

An array can also contain arrays inside. This is called multidimensional arrays.

Creating An Array

One Dimension Array

Let's take a look on how we can use arrays in our code. Arrays are created in a similar way to how we create a regular variable.

Syntax:

There are two ways to create an array:

```
var colors = new Array ("red", "blue", "yellow");
```

Or you may directly define it like this:

```
var colors = [red", "blue", "yellow"];
```

To assign and access the values inside an array, we refer to them by their element and index number. The numbers [0-2] in the sample below are the index numbers. The colors red, blue, and yellow are the corresponding array elements.

colors[0] = red
colors[1] = blue
colors[2] = yellow

You may also define an array name first and add values at a later time:

```
var colors = [];
colors[0]= "red";
colors[1]= "blue";
colors[2]= "yellow";
colors[55]= "green";
```

Note that in the above example, we have added the array element *green* to array index 55. Defining array indices sequentially is not required. However, this will automatically create blank elements from all the indices from 3 to 54. When you check on the array length, this will return 56 even if you only have 4 elements defined.

While you may create a long list of color names for your array, keep in mind that the maximum number of values an array can store is up to 4,294,967,295 elements.

Multidimensional Array

An array can contain an array containing an array. This can go on to several levels, depending on how you want to group your data.

Continuing with our *color* variable, follow the example below. Suppose that we want to store primary colors and secondary colors in this array.

Syntax:

To define multidimensional arrays, we use additional brackets to denote array and index number. Think of multidimensional arrays as outlines.

```
var color =
[["red","blue","yellow"],["green","purple","or
ange"]]
```

Using Arrays within the code

Retrieving array values

Use the code below to retrieve values from the sample above:

```
color[0][0];  //red
color[1][1];  //purple
   color[0];              //["red", "blue",
"yellow"]
```

Note in the last command that when you do not specify the specific index number when retrieving values for a multidimensional array, all of the array elements will be returned.

Array Properties

The array object comes with different properties.

Property	Description
prototype	Allows you to add properties and methods to an Array object
constructor	Ouputs a reference to the function that created the Array object
index	Zero-based index of the match in the string
input	Present only in arrays created by regular expression matches
length	Ouputs or sets the number of elements in an array

Here we demonstrate the different properties. Use the codes below to demonstrate the array properties.

Constructor

Syntax:

```
array.constructor
```

Exercise:

```
<html>
<head>
<title> constructor Property</title>
</head>
<body>
<script type="text/javascript">
   var samplearr = new Array( 15, 25,
35 );
   document.write("samplearr.construc
tor is:" + samplearr.constructor);
</script>
</body>
   </html>
```

Output:

```
samplearr.constructor is:function
Array() { [native code] }
```

Length

Syntax:

```
array.length
```

Exercise:

```
<html>
<head>
    <title> length Property</title>
</head>
    <body>
    <script type="text/javascript">
            var samplearr = new Array(
15, 25, 35 );
        document.write("samplearr.length
is:" + samplearr.length); </script>
</body>
</html>
```

Output:

```
samplearr.length is:3
```

Prototype

Syntax:

```
object.prototype.name = value
```

Exercise:

```html
<!DOCTYPE html>
<html>
<head>
<script type="text/javascript">
<!--
function book (title, author){
  this.title = title;
  this.author  = author;
}
//-->
</script>
</head>
<body>
  <script type="text/javascript">
  var myBook = new book("GOT",
"Martin");
  book.prototype.price=null;
  myBook.price=100;
  document.write("Book title is: " +
myBook.title + "<br>");
  document.write("Book author is: "
+ myBook.author + "<br>");
  document.write("Book price is: " +
myBook.price + "<br>");
  </script>
</body>
</html>
```

Output:

```
Book title is: GOT
Book author is: Martin
Book price is: 100
```

125

Array Methods

The following are the methods of the array object, including their description.

Method	Description
concat()	Ouputs a new array comprised of the given array joined with other arrays
every()	Ouputs true if every element in this array satisfies the test function
filter()	Creates a new array with all of the elements as long as the function used to filter function ouputs true.
forEach()	Calls a function for each array element
indexOf()	Outputs the first index of an array element equal to the given value
join()	Joins all elements of an array into one string
lastIndex Of()	Outputs the last index of an array element equal to the given value
map()	Generates a new array as a result of calling a function on every array element.
pop()	Deletes the last element from an array and outputs the element
push()	Adds one or more elements to the end of an array and outputs the new length of the array

reduce()	Apply a function simultaneously against two values of the array (from left-to-right)
reduceRight()	Apply a function simultaneously against two values of the array (from right-to-left)
reverse()	Reverses the order of the array elements
shift()	Removes the first element from an array and outputs that element.
slice()	Extracts a section of an array and returns a new array
some()	Outputs true if at least one array element satisfies the provided testing function
toSource()	Represents the source code of an object
sort()	Sorts the array elements
splice()	Adds and/or removes array elements
toString()	Returns a string representing array elements
unshift()	Adds one or more elements to the front of an array and outputs the new length of the array.

In the following exercises, we will explore how some of the array methods can be used:

concat()

Outputs a new array consisting of this array joined more arrays

Syntax:

```
array.concat(value1, value2, ...,
valueX);
```

Argument Details:

valueX : Arrays and/or values to concatenate to the resulting array.

Return Value:

Returns the array elements

Exercise:

```html
<html>
<head>
<title> Array concat </title>
</head>
<body>
<script type="text/javascript">
    var alphabet = ["x", "y", "z"];
    var numerals = [4, 5, 6];
    var alphaNumeric =
alphabet.concat(numerals);
        document.write("alphaNumeric : " +
alphaNumeric ); </script>
</body>
</html>
```

Output:

```
alphaNumeric : x,y,z,4,5,6
```

join()

Joins all the array elements into one string

Syntax:

```
array.join(delimiter);
```

Argument Details:

delimeter : Identifies a string that will separate each array element. If this is not defined, a comma will separate the array elements.

Exercise:

```
<html>
<head>
<title> Array join </title>
</head>
<body>
<script type="text/javascript">
    var Alphabet = new
Array("X","Y","Z");
    var newstring = Alphabet.join();
    ocument.write("new string : " +
newstring);
    var str = Alphabet.join(", ");
    document.write("<br /> new string
: " + newstring);
    var str = Alphabet.join(" + ");
    document.write("<br /> new string
: " + newstring);
</script>
</body>
</html>
```

Output:

```
new str : X,Y,Z
new str : X, Y, Z
new str : X + Y + Z
```

push()

Adds the given element in the last of the array and outputs the length of the new array

Syntax:
```
array.push();
```

Argument Details:

element1, ..., elementX: The elements to add to the end of the array.

Return Value:

Outputs the length of the new array.

Exercise:

```
<html>
<head>
<title> Array push </title> </head>
<body>
<script type="text/javascript">
    var numbers = new Array(2, 4,
6);
    var length = numbers.push(8);
document.write("new numbers are : " +
numbers );
        length = numbers.push(10);
    document.write("<br />new numbers is
: " + numbers ); </script>
</body>
</html>
```

Output:

```
new numbers are : 2,4,6,8
new numbers are : 2,4,6,8,10
```

reverse()

Reverses the element of an array

Syntax:

```
array.reverse();
```

Return Value:

Ouputs the length of the new array

Exercise:

```
<html>
<head>
<title> Array reverse </title>
</head>
<body>
  <script type="text/javascript">
  var num = [7, 8, 9, 10].reverse();
  document.write("Reversed array is
: " + num ); </script>
</body>
</html>
```

Output:

```
Reversed array is : 10, 9, 8, 7
```

shift()

Deletes the first element from an array and outputs that element.

Syntax:

```
array.shift();
```

Return Value:

Outputs the deleted single value of the array.

Exercise:

```html
<html>
<head>
<title> Array shift </title> </head>
<body>
<script type="text/javascript">
        var shiftelement = [123, 4, 5,
6].shift();
        document.write("Removed number is :
" + shiftelement ); </script>
</body>
```

Output:

```
Removed number is : 123
```

***

This is the last chapter of our JavaScript Beginner lessons. In the next chapter, I will give you more exercises that you can practice on.

Chapter Eleven: JavaScript Exercises

In this chapter, we will summarize all the basic concepts taught above by practicing on different exercises.

Exercise #1:

Display the current day and time according to the format specified below.

Sample Output:

```
Today is : Friday.
Current time is : 4 PM : 50 : 22
```

Solution:

```
<!DOCTYPE html>
  <html>
  <head>
  <meta charset="utf-8">
  <title>current day and time</title>
  </head>
  <body>
      <script type="text/javascript">
      var daytoday = new Date();
      var day = today.getDay();
      var allday =
["Sunday","Monday","Tuesday","Wednesday
","Thursday","Friday","Saturday"];
      console.log("Today is : " + allday[day] +
".");
      var dayhour = daytoday.getHours();
      var dayminute = daytoday.getMinutes();
      var daysecond = daytoday.getSeconds();
      var prep = (dayhour >= 12)? " PM ":" AM ";
      dayhour = (dayhour >= 12)? dayhour - 12:
dayhour;
      if (dayhour===0 && prep===' PM ')
          {
              if (dayminute===0 &&
daysecond===0)
              {
                  dayhour=12;
                  prep=' Noon';
              }
          else
              {
                  dayhour=12;
                  prep=' PM';
              }
          }
      if (dayhour===0 && prep===' AM ')
          {
              if (dayminute===0 &&
daysecond===0)
                  {
                      dayhour=12;
                      prep=' Midnight';
                  }
          else
              {
                  dayhour=12;
                  prep=' AM';
              }
```

```
        }
        console.log("Current Time : "+dayhour +
    prep + " : " + dayminute + " : " + daysecond);
</script>
</body>
</html>
```

Exercise #2:

Write a JavaScript function that reverses a number.

Sample Data and output:

```
Example x = 456;
Expected Output : 654
```

Solution:

```
<!DOCTYPE html>
  <html>
  <head>
  <meta charset="utf-8">
  <title>Reverse numbers</title>
  </head>
  <body>
      <script type="text/javascript">
      function reverse_number(n)
{
    n = n + "";
    return n.split("").reverse().join("");
}
alert(reverse_number(456));
</script>
</body>
</html>
```

Exercise #3:

Write a program that receives inputs of two integers and outputs the larger number.

Sample Data and output:

```
Example first integer = 100;
Example second integer = 500;
Expected Output : 500
```

Solution:

```html
<!DOCTYPE html>
  <html>
  <head>
  <meta charset="utf-8">
  <title>Compare integers</title>
  </head>
  <body>
      <script type="text/javascript">
      var num1, num2;
      yournumber1 = window.prompt("Enter your First
integer", "0");
      yournumber2 = window.prompt("Enter your second
integer", "0");
      if(parseInt(yournumber1, 10) >
parseInt(yournumber2, 10))
      {
            alert("The larger number between "+
yournumber1 + " and "+ yournumber2+ " is "+
yournumber1 + ".");
      }
      else
            if(parseInt(yournumber2, 10) >
parseInt(yournumber1, 10))
      {
            alert("The larger number between "+
yournumber1 +" and "+ yournumber2 + " is "+
yournumber2+ ".");
      }
      else
      {
            alert("The two values "+ yournumber1 + "
      and "+ yournumber2 + " are equal.");
      }
</script>
</body>
</html>
```

Exercise #4:

Write a JavaScript program to display the fruits in the following way:

Here is the sample array:
color = ["Apples ", "Oranges", "Grapes", "Pears", "Berries", "Peaches", "Bananas"];
a = ["th","st","nd","rd"]

Sample output:

```
"1st choice is Apples."
"2nd choice is Oranges."
"3rd choice is Grapes."
```

Solution:

```
<!DOCTYPE html>
  <html>
  <head>
  <meta charset="utf-8">
  <title>Color Array</title>
  </head>
  <body>
      <script type="text/javascript">
      var color = ["Apples ", "Oranges", "Grapes",
"Pears", "Berries", "Peaches", "Bananas"];
      function numbering(n)
      {
              var a = ["th","st","nd","rd"],
              x = n%100;
              return x+(o[(x-20)%10]||o[x]||o[0]);
      }

              for(n = 0; n < color.length; n++){
              var numbering = n + 1;
              var output = (numbering(numbering) + "
choice is " + color[n] + ".");

      console.log(output);
}
</script>
</body>
</html>
```

Exercise #5:

Write a Bubble Sort algorithm.
Note: Bubble sort is a simple sorting algorithm that works by repeatedly going through the list.

Sample Data : [10,7,0, 3,2,-1]
Expected Output :
[-1, 0, 2, 3, 7, 10]

Solution:

```html
<!DOCTYPE html>
  <html>
  <head>
  <meta charset="utf-8">
  <title>Bubble sort</title>
  </head>
  <body>
      <script type="text/javascript">
      Array.prototype.bubbleSort_algo = function()
      {
              var done_sorting = false;
              while (!done_sorting)
                  {
                      done_sorting = true;
                      for (var n = 0; n <
this.length - 1; n++)
                          {
                              if (this[n] >
this[n+1])
                                  {
                                  var x = this[n+1];
                                  this[n+1] = this[n];
                                  this[n] = x;
                                  done_sorting = false;
                                  }
                          }
                  }
              return this;
          };
console.log([10,7,0, 3,2,-1].bubbleSort_algo());
</script>
</body>
</html>
```

Congratulations! You have now completed this step-by-step guide, and have gained tremendous knowledge on JavaScript!

Turn to the next page to see a quick recap of what we have covered in this book.

Here is a quick recap of what we covered in case you need a refresher on a certain step:

1. You now have an understanding of what JavaScript is and what it can do as a programming language.
2. You now know how to use JavaScript within HTML or CSS.
3. You learned how to create variables in your program.
4. You now understand operators and expressions and you can now make expressions to satisfy requirements.
5. You now know how to use different branches, loops, and flow control statements to create a better program.
6. You now know what functions are and you can now create your own function statements.
7. You learned how to create objects.
8. You now know JavaScript objects and what these system-defined objects can do.
9. You also learned how to work with multiple values using arrays.
10. You can now write a short program of your own.

Turn to the next page to gain access to a free video course and to also see my other best-selling books part of this series!

Before You Go

In this book, I have provided you with the basic knowledge that you will need to start your journey in programming using JavaScript. The different concepts taught here, such as functions, loops, branches, and objects will equip you with the skills that you need to create your first JavaScript project.

Also, continue practicing and taking on small projects to start improving your skills. Through the knowledge imparted in this book, coupled with practice, you will be able to work on building your own websites or coding your own projects.

In your further study, I recommend that you learn and take on advanced topics such as troubleshooting in JavaScript, explore different frameworks and libraries, and expand your knowledge in using regular expressions.

I would also strongly recommend that you learn other programming languages so that you may be able to take your knowledge to the next level and become a top-class programmer. Because you have gone through this course, you will be astonished to find that learning other languages is easier than expected, for JavaScript has strikingly paved the way for you You can find other popular programming books by visiting our full library at >> http://amzn.to/1Xxmab2

I would now really appreciate your reviews and your feedback. If you really enjoyed this book, then feel free to share it so other people may also profit from this information.

Please visit http://amzn.to/1SRtCNy to leave a review!

Before You Go, Here Are Other Books Our Readers Loved!

Learn C Programming
Today With This Easy,
Step-By-Step Guide

★★★★★

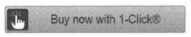

Learn R Programming
With This Easy,
Step-By-Step Guide

★★★★★

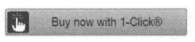

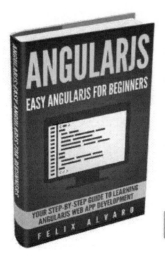

Learn AngularJS
Web-App Developing
Today With This Easy,
Step-By-Step Guide

★★★★★

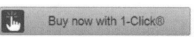

http://amzn.to/1pDq0BZ

Learn Java Programming
Today With This Easy,
Step-By-Step Guide!

★★★★★

http://amzn.to/1WTgUw0

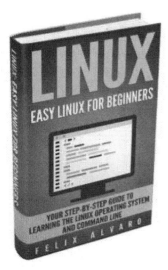

Learn The Linux Operating System and Command Line Today!

★★★★★

Buy now with 1-Click®

http://amzn.to/1QzQPkY

All You Need To Learn To Drive Tons Of Traffic To Your Website Today!

★★★★★

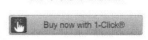

Buy now with 1-Click®

http://amzn.to/21HWFWb

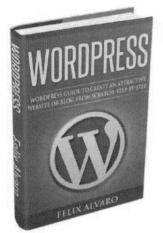

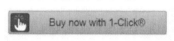

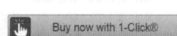

Finally, you can also send me an email if you have any questions, feedback or just want to say hello! (I do reply!) My email address is; (Felix_Alvaro@mail.com)

I thank you once again and God bless!

Felix Alvaro

19351619R00087

Printed in Poland
by Amazon Fulfillment
Poland Sp. z o.o., Wrocław